M

MW01093942

The Inspirational Story of Baseball Superstar Miguel Cabrera

Table of Contents

Introduction

As the title implies, this is a short book about [The Inspirational Story of Baseball Superstar Miguel Cabrera] and how he rose from his life in Venezuela to become one of today's leading and most-respected baseball players. In his rise to superstardom, Miguel has inspired not only the youth, but fans of all ages throughout the world.

This book also portrays the key moments Miguel had to go through during his early childhood years, his teen years, until he became what he is today. A notable source of inspiration is Cabrera's service to the community and his strong connection with the fans of the sport. He continues to serve as the jovial character who loves to play the superstar role and prove doubters wrong every time he steps on the field.

Combining incredible strength, extreme patience at the plate, quick bat speed, and superior coordination, Miguel has shown the ability to change the outcome of any game. From being a young boy in Venezuela to becoming one of the greatest baseball players of his generation, you'll learn how this man has risen to the ranks of the best baseball players in the game.

Thanks again for grabbing this book. Hopefully you can take inspiration and lessons from Miguel's story and apply them to your own life!

Chapter 1:

Youth

The life of Jose Miguel Torres Cabrera was always closely associated with baseball. Miguel's parents were great players during their youth. The two met on the baseball field, fell in love, and started a family.

His father, also named Miguel, was a highly touted amateur player in the country of Venezuela. However, his professional career did not pan out as he would have liked. He has since studied engineering and earned his keep by running his own auto shop.

His mother, Gregoria, was the Venezuelan softball national team shortstop for more than a decade. After fourteen years of pursuing her passion, Gregoria became a teacher. She tutored children in her hometown of Maracay, Venezuela. Her brother and Miguel's late uncle, David Torres, was likewise an athlete. David was signed by the St. Louis Cardinals but only reached the Class AA level.

Miguel's other uncle, Jose Torres, was also involved in baseball. He also helped in training a young Miguel Cabrera, in Maracay. Jose still lives in the same house, right next to where Miguel grew up. Jose now operates a baseball training school founded by his late brother, David.

Miguel, or Miggy, as he is fondly called, was born on April 18th, 1983 in Maracay, Venezuela. The family lived a simple life. He, with his parents and sibling, lived in in the La Padrera neighborhood, one of the poorer sections of Maracay. They occupied a small two-bedroom house with a kitchen and one bathroom. Miggy shared a room with his younger sister, Ruth, while their parents took the other one. They were in a small community comprised of five other families, all of whom were relatives. The Cabrera brood eventually moved to a more prosperous neighborhood after Miguel made it big. The rest of the clan, including his grandmother, still calls that simple part of Maracay their home.

Needless to say, Miguel was exposed to baseball at a young age. He would tag along to watch his mother's baseball games. When he was not in the dugout, Miguel would play tune-up games with his father or uncle. If he was not doing any of these, he would sneak into games at the nearby Maracay Stadium by simply climbing the fence that separated the baseball field and the family's backyard. Cabrera's fascination and cheerfulness for the game was planted during his childhood, and to this day, he looks like a kid while playing in the majors.

Outside of baseball, Miguel spent a lot of time with his sister, Ruth, and was an obedient son to his parents. The Cabreras have a close-knit family, and both Miguel and Ruth rewarded their parents by doing well in school. But Miguel got into trouble, like any other boy his age. He used to hang out with a rowdy bunch of kids. Fistfights were common back then. They would play baseball one minute and exchange punches the next.

Miguel also got teased for his relatively large head. His friends used to call him *cabeza tren* or train head. Whenever they called him names, he would get mad, but he seldom lashed out at them. Miguel kept his emotions bottled up. If he got angry at his friends, they would tease him more. His only option was to ignore the name calling and check his emotions. His penchant for bottling his emotions stayed with him as he grew up. It is evident in how he dislikes interviews and prefers to keep things to himself as a professional.

Family and baseball were practically all that young Miguel had back then, because he grew up in the most impoverished area of his hometown. Because they had little money to spare, the siblings would practice using a round stick as a bat and piles of paper for gloves. During this time, Miguel also learned to play basketball and volleyball, but ultimately, baseball was his true love.

Since he was exposed to the sport at such a young age and came from a family that excelled in it, Miguel's early baseball talent was innate, and it was gradually brought out during his teen years. He played organized baseball at six and word about his prowess on the diamond spread throughout town. Aside from learning by himself, his uncle David became a mentor, and they would work together almost every day, until David passed away in 1997 of a heart attack.

Miguel learned more than just baseball from his late uncle. David also imparted his wisdom, regarding North American baseball and the dangers that would come with it.

Miguel fueled his fascination with baseball by following the career of Cincinnati Reds shortstop and fellow Venezuelan, Dave Concepcion, who also hails from Maracay. The Reds were one of Major League Baseball's top teams during the 1970s, and Concepcion was one of the team's stars. Indirectly, the teenager, Cabrera, was so motivated by Concepcion's rise that he eventually became a better prospect than his idol. It was also around this time that scouts from major league teams took notice of Miguel's work ethic, precise batting, and his powerful swing.

Even though he had what it takes to be a successful professional baseball player, Miguel's father wanted him to be an engineer, just like him. As previously mentioned, the older Miguel once had a promising baseball career that did not pan out in the majors. He found another profession and he did not want the same disappointment to happen to his son. However, the younger Miguel's will to chase his dream could not be broken. Miguel's father supported his dream, granted he would get his high school diploma first.

Little is known regarding Miguel's academic schooling career, but we know he was an exceptional player while in grade school. He was already competing in national baseball competitions at six. From there, his career continually prospered, so much so, that Major League Baseball teams were already courting him while he was in high school.

With an entourage of supporters and scouts following him, it must have been a struggle for him to focus on school life. Despite this potential distraction, he played well for his school and gained his high school diploma, which his father requested before he turned professional.

The teams that showed genuine interest in Cabrera were the Minnesota Twins, the New York Yankees, the Los Angeles Dodgers, and the

Florida Marlins. When he was just 15 years old, Cabrera tried out for then-Marlins scout Louie Eljaua. The scout was impressed. Eljaua informed Al Avila, the scouting director, of this Venezuelan kid with arms like cannons and a spring-loaded bat. Avila quickly flew in and watched Miguel play. He, too, was overly impressed and told Dombrowski, then the Florida GM, about the young phenomenon.

Miguel was inclined to sign with the Marlins, but the financial commitment that the Dodgers and the Yankees would make was tempting. But in July of 1999, Miguel officially became a professional baseball player at 16, by signing a minor league contract with the Marlins for $1.8 million. Miguel also chose the team because of their commitment to developing young Latin American players, such as Livan Hernandez and Edgar Renteria.

Chapter 2:

Professional Life

After signing with the Marlins, Miguel moved to the United States. He lived in an apartment in Florida with five other A-ball players from Latin America. It was a difficult time for Miguel. He was in a new place with people he didn't know. Even worse, he didn't speak English. Something simple like getting a bite to eat could become a drag. All he ate during his early days were Meal No. 3 of Burger King, just because it was the easiest thing to say.

And when the person behind the counter would ask him if he wanted fries or what size he wanted his drink to be, his answer would always be the same – "yes". As Miguel was working on his baseball skills, he enrolled in an English class to help make his transition to America easier. He

Chapter 2:

Professional Life

After signing with the Marlins, Miguel moved to the United States. He lived in an apartment in Florida with five other A-ball players from Latin America. It was a difficult time for Miguel. He was in a new place with people he didn't know. Even worse, he didn't speak English. Something simple like getting a bite to eat could become a drag. All he ate during his early days were Meal No. 3 of Burger King, just because it was the easiest thing to say.

And when the person behind the counter would ask him if he wanted fries or what size he wanted his drink to be, his answer would always be the same – "yes". As Miguel was working on his baseball skills, he enrolled in an English class to help make his transition to America easier. He also read lots of newspapers to hone is understanding of the language.

Before joining the Marlins' farm team in the Gulf Coast League, Miguel forewent college to play in the Venezuelan Winter Baseball League. After a year, he joined the Gulf Coast League Marlins as a shortstop, wherein he teamed up with the likes of Dontrelle Willis and Adrian Gonzalez. In 57 games with the GCL Marlins, Miguel compiled an impressive stat line of a .260 batting average with two home runs, two triples, and ten doubles.

This prompted a promotion to Class-A baseball, where Miguel would play eight games with the New York-Penn League Blue Sox of Utica, New York. In his short stint, Miguel amassed a .250 batting average and had six runs batted in (RBIs). From there, he climbed the ranks to Low Class A baseball and played for the Kane Country Cougars of Geneva, Illinois, where he once again teamed up with Adrian Gonzalez. Miguel's numbers with Kane were impressive: .260 average, 66 RBI and 30 multiple-base hits. His steady play merited a stint in the MLB All-Star Weekend Futures Game. He was also regarded for having the strongest arm in the Midwest League.

By the following season, Miguel was promoted to High Class A and played for the Jupiter Hammerheads of the Florida State League. Here, he was coached by former Major League player and manager, Ozzie Guillen, who converted him to third base. Again, Miguel played in the Futures Game and finished the season with a .278 batting average to go with 75 RBI and 30 multiple-base hits.

In 2003, Miguel climbed the ranks to Class AA and suited up for the Carolina Mudcats, while teaming up, once again, with Dontrelle Willis. It was in this stint that Miguel truly showed an MLB-ready form by tallying a .365 batting average with 10 home runs and 59 RBI. From that stat line, Miguel had shaken off his home run woes by increasing his total. Therefore, this stint started him as the reliable clean-up hitter he would become in his future years.

The Florida Marlins were loaded with talented guys, such as catcher Pudge Rodriguez, pitcher Josh Beckett, shortstop Alex Gonzalez, Derek Lee at first base, Luis Castillo taking care of second base, Mike Lowell at third, and Juan Pierre at centerfield. However, injuries were taking its toll on the team's chemistry. The potentially playoff bound team was languishing in the middle of the pack and was likely to fall further.

The club was searching for a spark, so they looked to Willis for help. With Willis to the big league, it still wasn't enough to change the team's fortune. The franchise continued reshuffling, even in the front office, as they let go of Jeff Torborg, the Marlins manager, and replaced him with Jack McKeon. While things started to pick up, it still wasn't enough to make management happy. That's when the front office tried its luck on Miguel.

Some in the organization thought Cabrera wasn't ready yet at the time of his call up. While he trained and learned how to shift position to left field while with the Mudcats, there was much space for improvement. Enter Andre "The Hawk" Dawson. The former NL MVP, who currently works in the Marlins front office, took Cabrera under his wing and showed him how to properly play left field.

By the age of 20, Miguel had officially moved up to play in Major League Baseball. However, no one could have imagined how he would take the league by storm. Miggy officially joined the Florida Marlins on June 20th. This made him the second youngest player to play his first Major League game for the Marlins. The "Barranquilla Baby", Edgar Renteria, was only 19 when he debuted with the franchise. Miguel's first game was against the Tampa Bay Devil Rays.

Miguel quickly made a name for himself in his first game. He connected on a walk-off home run, making him only the third player since 1900, to hit a game-winning walk-off homer in his big league debut.

Miguel continued to perform well throughout his rookie season, especially after he became the designated cleanup batter. He would contribute heavily to the Marlins' World Series title at the end of the season. He helped the team reach the World Series and win over the New York Yankees, 4-2. His most memorable at-bat during his rookie season was the two-run home run he drilled against Roger Clemens in Game 4 of the World Series, to tie the series at two games apiece. Miguel considers that one of his fondest memories. What made it more memorable was he wasn't scared, even one bit, when he faced off against the legend. Not even after Clemens threw a fastball that almost grazed Miggy's chin. Not even after two strikes, a ball, and two foul-offs. He just shrugged it off and went to work. This poise for such a young player is rare.

Miguel hit an impressive .286 during the National League Division Series against the Giants. He was even better during the NL Conference Series, with .333 hit and three home runs to his credit against the Chicago Cubs. For the season, Miguel finished with a .268 average, highlighted by 12 home runs and 62 RBI. Those figures were good enough to lead the whole team.

The following season, his excellent performance (33 home runs, 112 RBI, 177 hits, .294 batting average, and .512 sluggish percentage) earned him a spot in the All-Star Game, his first selection. In 2005, he placed second, with 198 total hits among National League players. He also posted a .323 batting average to go with 43 doubles, two triples, and 116 RBI.

Miggy also had 33 home runs, making him the youngest player to hit at least 30 home runs in two consecutive seasons, and he did this during his first couple of seasons in the League. Miguel was later awarded with his first Silver Slugger Award and a spot in the MLB All-Star Game.

Before the season started, Miguel was chosen to be part of the Venezuelan national team that played in the World Baseball Classic. Even with Cabrera on board, the team finished a disappointing seventh, while Japan took home the trophy.

Miguel played for the Florida Marlins until the 2006-2007 season. He improved consistently, finishing with a batting average of .339, with 26 homers, 114 RBI, and a .568 slugging percentage. He won his second Silver Slugger Award and participated in his third All-Star Game. He also took part in his first Home Run Derby. He hit 15 homers for third place.

Miguel continued his journey to superstardom with his 500th career RBI in his 2007 season. He was the third youngest player to reach that mark, after Mel Ott and Ted Williams. He was again voted into the All-Star Game and the Home Run Derby, though he played limited minutes in the former and skipped the latter due to an injury.

On December 5th, 2007, Miguel was traded to the Detroit Tigers, along with Dontrelle Willis. The trade involved Cabrera and Willis swapping teams with four pitchers (Dallas Trahern, Burke Badenhop, Andrew Miller, Eulogio dela Cruz), an outfielder (Cameron Maybin), and a catcher (Mike Rabelo).

Miguel still remembers how he felt after learning about the trade. It was December then, and he was driving. He got a call from his GM, who told him he was being traded to the Tigers. Miggy didn't want to leave Florida. He was finally comfortable there. But all they could say to him was that was how the League and professional sports works.

In March of 2008, Miguel signed an eight-year, $152.3 million contract, which was the fourth largest contract in the league at that time. In his first year as a Tiger, Miguel showed he was worth it by posting a .292 batting average to go with 37 home runs and over 100 RBI.

After a stint with Venezuela in the 2009 World Baseball Classic, Miguel channeled his momentum into another fine MLB season. In his second year with the Detroit Tigers, Miguel amassed a .324 batting average on 198 hits and, once again, had over 100 RBI. He maintained his form into the next season, when he finished with a .328 batting average, a career-high 38 homers, and 126 RBI. However, he led the American League in errors among first basemen, with 13.

In 2011, Miguel grabbed the American League batting title by hitting an average of .344. He also recorded 30 home runs and 105 RBI for the year. Cabrera led the American League in on-base percentage and walks that year with .448 and 48, respectively. By this point, Miguel was considered one of the best offensive players in the game, without a doubt.

Before the start of the 2012-2013 season, Miguel was struck just below his right eye by a ground ball, hit by Hunter Pence of the Philadelphia Phillies. The injury raised concerns that Miguel might have to miss significant games the following season, but he was able to start on Opening Day after the team's orbital surgeon cleared him.

In his finest season in Major League Baseball, Miguel Cabrera registered a .330 batting average, with 44 home runs and 139 RBI, good enough to take home the Triple Crown award. He was also named American League MVP. It was one of the greatest offensive seasons baseball has ever seen. However, the season ended with the Tigers suffering a 4-0 World Series defeat to the San Francisco Giants.

Miguel would continue to accumulate even more accolades during the 2013-2014 season, including a third straight American League batting crown, with a .348 batting average. He also won a second consecutive AL MVP award for his success. Aside from his statistical accomplishments, Miguel was also the Tigers' nominee for the Roberto Clemente Award in 2012 and 2013 for being the player who best represented the sport, on and off the diamond.

During the 2014 season, Miguel recorded his 2,000th career hit. He was the seventh youngest in MLB history to reach the milestone. Miguel's fan support was strong as ever, as he was voted into his ninth All-Star Game, and chosen as the starting AL first baseman for the second year in a row. He also extended his streak of at least 100 RBI in consecutive seasons to eleven, placing him on par with legends Lou Gehrig, Jimmie Foxx, Alex Rodriguez, and Al Simmons. After recording his 100th RBI, Miguel earned the AL Player of the Week award, the 11th in his career, and later, the AL Player of the Month for September.

Miggy ended the season leading the League with 52 doubles and in sacrifice flies, with eleven. He also had a batting average of .313, good for 10th place, 109 RBI (third), and 25 home runs. He became only the fourth big leaguer to finish with at least 20 homers, 30 doubles, 80 runs, and 75 RBI for nine seasons in a row. One more season with such statistics, and he'd equal Stan Musial, Manny Ramirez, and Albert Pujols, with 10 consecutive seasons each to their credit.

Miguel was nominated for his first Gold Glove Award for first base, but lost to Eric John Hosmer of the Kansas City Royals, the previous year's winner. That was not his only setback for 2014. Miguel had been suffering from pain in his right foot for months, particularly during the latter half of the season. This forced him to change the mechanics of his swing, so his right foot wouldn't feel the brunt of his weight. A day after his nomination, Miguel had a bone spur in his right ankle removed through surgery. During the operation, his doctors discovered a stress fracture in his navicular bone, also on his right foot.

Miguel has been a durable player throughout his career, one who has lost little time due to injuries. His stubbornness to play through the pain in his right foot is a testament to his perseverance and love for the game. The longest span of games he's missed during a season was fourteen, due to a groin surgery to remove a sports hernia.

The 2015 season saw Miguel become the all-time leader in home runs among Venezuelan players to have played in MLB. This is quite a feat, as there are 321 current and former players, by last count, who hail from the Latin American country. Among these legendary Venezuelans are the "Big Cat" Andres Galarraga, who previously held the distinction, the Big Red Machine's Hall of Famer Dave Concepcion, Cy Young awardee Johan Santana, former Tiger teammate Magglio Ordonez, and Omar Vizquel, who at 45 became the oldest player in history to play shortstop, in 2012.

Miguel recorded his 400th career home run on May 16th, 2015 at 32 years and 28 days of age, the eighth youngest in League history to do so. His homer against the St. Louis Cardinals' Tyler Lyons also placed him third youngest among active players, behind Albert Pujols and Alex Rodriguez.

Chapter 3:

Personal Adult Life

Every fan knows Miguel Cabrera, the baseball player. Little is known about Miguel Cabrera, the person. While he is one of the most recognizable faces in the world of baseball, Miggy has never opened up about his personal life, particularly his childhood. If you are an outsider, a fan maybe, you know Miguel is a quiet guy. If he doesn't know you personally, you're lucky to get more than two words at a time from him. He's not particularly fond of interviews or the limelight. But being, arguably, the best baseball player in his generation, the period after the proliferation of steroids and other performance-enhancing drugs, it is difficult to shun his celebrity status.

Miguel is a different man with his close associates, however. His teammates don't see him as the shy person everybody thinks he is. He warms up to teammates. He's known among them to come to work always with a smile on his face and a lot of positivity and goofiness in his persona.

Miggy is no diva. In 2012, he made the move from first baseman to third base to accommodate free agent signee, Prince Fielder, who had played that position throughout his career. Cabrera didn't bat an eye when the move was made. He was happy to do so. What is more impressive is that Miguel wasn't bothered that the new Tiger earned more than he did. Fielder was signed to a nine-year, $214 million contract, while Cabrera's contract was a "meager" $185.3 million in eight years. Fielder was overly thankful and impressed with Cabrera's sacrifice. Fielder has since been traded to the Texas Rangers for Ian Kinsler after two disappointing seasons.

One difference between the superstar, baseball hero Miggy from the young, naive Miggy is he now travels with bodyguards, especially when he goes home to Maracay. His home country has seen no, proverbial, light at the end of the tunnel lately. It has been embroiled in bankruptcy and crisis after crisis in recent years.

The International Monetary Fund (IMF) estimated the country's 2015 economic growth was -10%, the worst in the world. The inflation rate is high. The crime rate, especially murders, has increased dramatically. The country ranked second with the highest crime rate in the world next to South Sudan. The government has even extended the Easter holiday and ordered the people not to go to work for five more days just to conserve power.

This culmination of circumstances has led to the withdrawal of numerous scouts from MLB. From a high of 20 teams represented by several scouts in the country, only four, as of 2015, remain. There have been incidents of gang fights starting near the scouts. The Seattle Mariners academy, now abandoned, was the target of some criminals after scouts and players were robbed at gunpoint.

In 2011, catcher Wilson Ramos of the Washington Nationals was kidnapped by four armed men right outside his home in Valencia, Venezuela. After two days, Ramos was rescued, while eight men were arrested. When Miguel goes back to visit his childhood community, even the police chime in. The police escorts and bodyguards stay outside their home to give them some privacy. Miggy is just playing it safe, as the threat is quite real.

Miguel tried other sports, particularly basketball and volleyball, during his youth. As an adult, he's tried golf and archery. He quit playing golf after some time because he didn't get the hang of it. Even the hardworking Cabrera cannot excel in everything he tries, and that is something he can't readily accept.

According to the baseball superstar, he doesn't "want to be second best". That is why he worked hard to perfect being a third baseman. Former Tigers General Manager Dave Dombrowski described Cabrera as someone who doesn't like to be embarrassed. Because his golfing skills were getting so embarrassing, he shifted to archery, where his hawk-like vision has come in handy.

Nevertheless, baseball remains Cabrera's unrivaled passion. His goal in life is to be the best at his craft. With his hard work and determination, not surprisingly, he's on the baseball pedestal. His knowledge of the game is also incomparable. He studies every pitcher. He spends a lot of time studying their hitting charts.

There's even a rumor that Miguel knows every pitch in every starting pitcher's arsenal. His brilliant mind is also his greatest weakness, at least, according to his wife, Rosangel. He's been told he likes to overthink. Rosangel even said that Miguel doesn't listen to her when she speaks, but will be in his own world, thinking, when talking to someone else. His overthinking is the main reason he doesn't waste time watching game tapes.

Another of Miguel's passions is movies. Rosangel has a lot to do with this passion of his. When he was still in Venezuela, he met a young Rosangel. He courted the pretty girl, who eventually became his girlfriend. Most of their dates were spent at the theater watching films. Miguel, eventually, had to leave the country, but returned six years later to ask for Rosangel's hand. He was making a name for himself at that time, as he was playing for the Marlins.

However, Rosangel's parents were opposed to the marriage. But the star-crossed lovers wouldn't let their youth and her parents get in the way. They were married in 2002 and moved to the United States. Since then, the young couple spends most of their free time watching movies. They go to movie houses on dates. They collect DVDs as well, with Miguel preferring comedy films, while his wife likes horror thrillers.

Miguel was only 22 when they had their first daughter, Rosangel, who they affectionately call Brisel. Their love has also brought them another daughter, Isabella, and a son, Christopher Alexander. Another great quality of Miguel's is his genuine affection towards children. When his first daughter was born, he remembers being so fidgety and excited to play with Brisel.

Miggy also loved to play with his young cousins. Their favorite game was paper baseball. Back in the field, he used to play with Dombrowski's son, Langdon. Miguel could be seen goofing around with his former GM's son, who is now a teenager. He is a child at heart.

One of Miguel's favorite places in the world is Disneyland. He and his friends in Venezuela used to dream of going to the famous theme park. Now that he's made it in America, he can go see Mickey Mouse and the rest of the gang whenever he wants. He likes to "force" his teammates to go with him to the park.

Miguel has had to overcome some excessive alcohol drinking problems during his time as an adult. However, he's worked hard to get his issues under control. He did not participate in the festivities for clinching the division title against the Kansas City Royals, even though some of the champagne served that night was non-alcoholic.

Many people who struggle with alcohol addiction look up to Cabrera as a role model because of his strong desire to overcome his personal issues with alcohol. Although it hasn't always been easy, and he has definitely made mistakes in his journey to overcoming excessive drinking, his effort cannot go unquestioned.

That he checked himself in to a rehabilitation facility for three months is impressive for an athlete of his stature and fame. Most celebrities in similar situations are not willing to admit they have issues or choose not to take care of them because of their egos.

When Cabrera chose not to participate in the division clinching celebration to maintain his stance on alcohol related activities, it said a lot about his character. Moments like those are huge accomplishments for a professional athlete and not to be celebrating with your team to prevent relapse takes a lot of self-control and maturity.

Miguel practices both Catholicism and Santeria. In 2006, he became an official Santeria Babalawo, or father of mysticism. Within Santeria, it is a highly regarded title, only reserved for anointed priests of the Ifa divination system that represents the Spirit of Wisdom. They are spiritual guides, and at times, social advisors for those who practice Santeria. As a Babalawo, Miguel holds himself with high moral regard, which still holds true.

Chapter 4:

Philanthropies and Charitable Acts

In 2012, Miguel started a foundation with his name at the helm, to help develop the physical and leadership skills of youth through various enhancement programs, community ballpark construction, and leadership academies. His foundation has helped various individuals and communities in the United States, Latin America, and the Caribbean.

The foundation is based in Miami, Florida, and over its brief stint, has organized charity baseball games and tribute dinners to raise funds for its operations. Since Miguel is part of the franchise, this foundation works closely with the Detroit Tigers Foundation. Some of the foundation's benefactors are Merrill Lynch, General Motors,

Relativity Sports, Donald Moylan, and Leo Burnett.

In his old neighborhood, Miggy is not just known for his baseball exploits. He is also appreciated for his charitable acts. Remember that Venezuela has the worst economy in the world, so it may be easier to understand the people there need help. Though Cabrera would gamely help out, he prefers those who are struggling to learn how to overcome adversities and succeed in life, much like he did, when he was still living in Maracay.

Chapter 5:

Legacy and Inspiration for Others

Like many professional baseball players, the journey of Miguel Cabrera is a rags to riches story, wherein a man pursued his dream and achieved milestones beyond what he could conceive as a youngster. From an impoverished neighborhood in Venezuela, Miguel kept feeding his fascination with baseball by working with people who could help him improve, and having professional players he could look up to. Miguel used his talent as a ticket to a better life, and he keeps chasing more achievements, because he doesn't want the struggles of his old life back.

Back in his country, especially in his hometown of Maracay, the youngsters look to Miguel as an inspiration. Those who know him and his story proudly share how this poor, simple kid used his skills and talents to reach the pinnacle of success and become a household name. They also preach to the children that Cabrera focused on his studies, when not practicing on the diamond. He didn't stray too far from the right path. According to his uncle Jose, Miggy "erased from his life the things that could cause him to fail". Many elders within the community want their children to take this to heart.

There was a time when the family felt they were no longer at home in their own country and thought chasing the American dream was the best thing to do. But all wasn't how Miguel expected it to be when he arrived in America. He didn't belong. He was a stranger in a strange, new world. But as time went by, his dream came true. Thanks to perseverance, hard work, and honed skills on the baseball diamond, Miggy and the rest of his family accomplished what many have strived for.

His life is not perfect. He has brushed off several issues during his dominant career. However, his willingness to bounce back and keep on improving as a human being should serve as an inspiration for those who are saddled with challenges. He has sought help to make things right, and he has become the victor in multiple aspects of his life.

Finally, Miguel gives back to the people who supported him by setting up a foundation. He shows his gratefulness by giving others a chance to chase their dreams. In his hometown, he is a popular figure, not just because of his exploits on the diamond. Cabrera has helped his neighbors in any way he can. While acquiring so much by playing baseball, he has used some of it to plant a seed of hope for those chasing the same dream he did when he was a youngster.

From a troubled past, Miguel Cabrera has molded himself into a role model, on and off the diamond. He is a baseball superstar that a new generation of players can idolize. He understands that a lot of young individuals are looking up to him, and he has transformed himself as an ideal leader and a good man.

Conclusion

Hopefully this book helped you gain inspiration from the life of Miguel Cabrera, one of the best players in Major League Baseball.

The rise and fall of a star is often the cause for much wonder. But most stars have an expiration date. In baseball, once a star player reaches his mid- to late-thirties, it is often time to contemplate retirement. What will be left in people's minds about that fading star? In Miguel Cabrera's case, people will remember how he came onto the scene for the Marlins and Tigers and helped boost their team from mediocrity. He will be remembered as the guy who had some of the best years baseball has ever seen, across any era of the game.

Miguel has also inspired many people, because he is the star who never fails to connect with fans and continues to give back to communities around the world. Whether it is in Detroit, Miami, or his home in Venezuela, Miguel loves

Conclusion

Hopefully this book helped you gain inspiration from the life of Miguel Cabrera, one of the best players in Major League Baseball.

The rise and fall of a star is often the cause for much wonder. But most stars have an expiration date. In baseball, once a star player reaches his mid- to late-thirties, it is often time to contemplate retirement. What will be left in people's minds about that fading star? In Miguel Cabrera's case, people will remember how he came onto the scene for the Marlins and Tigers and helped boost their team from mediocrity. He will be remembered as the guy who had some of the best years baseball has ever seen, across any era of the game.

Miguel has also inspired many people, because he is the star who never fails to connect with fans and continues to give back to communities around the world. Whether it is in Detroit, Miami, or his home in Venezuela, Miguel loves

to share his success with those who are less fortunate. Lastly, he's remarkable for remaining simple and firm with his principles, despite his immense popularity.

Hopefully you've learned some great things about Miguel in this book and can apply the lessons and principles to your life! Good luck in your own journey!